KWANZAA

A Celebration of Family, Community, and Culture

FACT BOOK SECOND EDITION, 2022

Professor Tamu Chambers, author

Education and Social Sciences Department

Hudson Valley Community College

OrionPress
www.orionpressbooks.com
1382 Belmont Road, Raymond, WA98577

Table of Contents

Dear teachers,

The *Kwanzaa Fact Book* is dedicated to you and your students. Collectively educating students is a societal responsibility that we all share to model future scholars' humanity and intellect.

PREFACE

Over two decades ago, what is now the Education and Social Sciences Department, sponsored a Kwanzaa production on campus. The enthusiastic support from Dennis Nagi, department chair at the time, led the way. The Hudson Valley Community College's president and other key administrators were equally instrumental in making the event a successful learning experience for students, faculty and staff.

Collectively, we share the conviction that education should include student-centered learning activities, particularly as related to understanding the influences that culture, ethnicity, and diversity have on human thinking, feelingandbehavior.Many educators praise experiential learning exercises, which actively involve students in the learning process. We recognize that informed individuals can make choices more freely and can better resist social practices and attitudes that are prejudicial and unjust.

Although the event centered on an African American experience, the focus was to provide an educational and multicultural happening for all participants. Students of African, African American, European, Latino, Asian, Indian, and mixed heritage, as well as faculty and staff, were introduced to a celebration of African American culture. As a faculty member, it is a pleasure to respond to many requests from students for information about Kwanzaa. No experimental studies have assessed the efficacy of exercises such as the Kwanzaa production, there is every reason to believe that they are more effective teaching stools than a conventional lecture alone. Comments from students, faculty and staff support this theory.

Students' evaluations said: "The production heightens interest in lecture materials;" "It made the material more meaningful." Faculty and staff reported that it helped to refine and expand their understanding of Kwanzaa. Others said, "The ceremony provided opportunities to relate the material to broader contextualized settings."

Based on my classroom experiences and observations as a professor of cultural studies and sociology, students are frequently surprised by the omission of the information or experience of other groups, particularly African Americans. Much information is either neglected or under-reported in many texts. Many students are seeking greater understanding of various cultures. Limited space in the booklet allows minimal, but necessary information. Therefore, the selection is based upon student reaction from supplemental facts presented during class lectures.

The content in this Fact Book is written from a socio-historical perspective. It is my belief that knowledge of a group's history promotes understanding of the group's past, present and hopefully, a great future for those who are living it and enhanced understanding for those who are visiting cultural events or taking courses for a brief period. Consequently, a short introduction of the historic underpinnings of the social unrest is essential for understanding the importance of this cultural holiday. The information is organized in such a fashion to inform those who are aware of the socio-historical foundation leading up to this event. Those whose interests lie merely in the celebration, may fast forward to those sections.

INTRODUCTION

Review of the literature explains that Dr. Maulana Dabezitha Karenga (b. 1941), an African American scholar and social activist, is the father of Kwanzaa. During the 1970s, he earned his first of two doctorate degrees. Currently, he chairs the Black Studies Department at California State University at Long Beach. Though best known for institutionalizing African philosophy and culture on college campuses throughout the United States–the yearly Kwanzaa ("first fruit") celebration, Dr. Karenga also helped organize a number of Black Power conferences. He became involved in civil rights after the Watts riot of 1965 when he founded the cultural nationalist and social organization. U.S. Kwanzaa was established in 1966 as the only original African American, family-oriented holiday. It focuses on enhancing people's pride of family and community by embracing African traditions, customs, symbols, and language. Dr. Karenga developed his celebration as a response to social discord in the African American community.

Today, many African Americans celebrate Kwanzaa. Often, this increasingly popular holiday is either celebrated in conjunction with, or instead of Christmas. The celebration has spread from the United States to Canada, the Caribbean, Great Britain, France and Africa. Kwanzaa is a spiritual, festive and joyous celebration which claims no ties to any religion. It is a week of "remembering, reassessing and rejoicing." Dr. Karenga gives two reasons for the seven-day period, beginning on Dec. 26 and ending on Jan. 1. First, the schedule corresponds with the first fruit festivals in many parts of Africa. Second, it fits into the established pattern of year-end celebrations in the United States.

AFRICAN AMERICAN COMMUNITY

The Black family as a Social System

The family is embedded in a matrix of mutually interdependent relationships within the Black community and the wider society. And there are subsystems within the family: husband-wife, mother-son, father-daughter, grandmother-mother-daughter, and so forth.

The Black community includes schools, churches, lodges, social clubs, funeral societies, organized systems of hustling, and other institutions.

The wider society consists of major institutions: value, political, economic, health, welfare, and communication subsystems.
(Adapted from A. Billingsley, Black Families in White America, Englewood Cliffs, NJ: Prentice Hall,1968.)

A Socio-political Perspective

To understand the importance of Kwanzaa, a brief introduction of socio-historical political forces and the legalization of second class citizens of the "colored" people in American is recounted. Inspite of the Emancipation Proclamation of 1863, racism or the belief that some individuals, particularly African Americans, were born into a group with inferior intelligence, low morals and the inability to interact in society was deeply ingrained in the fabric of American society.

Events occurring throughout the 1950s and 1960s are viewed by many historians and sociologists as the pinnacle of the second Civil Rights Movement. The United States was a country in flames. Much social unrest in the Black communities stemmed from the triple evils of poverty. As pointed out by Dr. Martin Luther King (1929-1968), "poverty, racism and violence are evidence that America is reaching spiritual and moral death." Another poignant example of political, economic and social discord is found in the following quote by a renowned psychologist:

"The dark ghettos are social, political educational and – above all – economic colonies. Their inhabitants are subject peoples, victims of the greed, cruelty, insensitivity guilt and fear of their masters."
–Dr. Kenneth B. Clark (1914-2005), Dark Ghetto

Also, political discord became a point of contention among many leaders in the wider society, as well as within the vanguard of the African American community. Young college students became disenchanted and impatient with the pace of the movement and much of the philosophy emanating from the old vanguard. Slogans such as "we shall overcome" were being replaced by "we shall overrun."

In the '60s, many cities consisting of large black populations were on fire. Property destruction and personal injuries were part of the daily lives of many residing in the inner cities. Fires flickered from Watts/Los Angeles in California to Detroit, Michigan to Harlem in New York City to Newark, New Jersey. In the aftermath of the riots, many African Americans in Watts and across the city joined with a purpose to rebuild Watts and make the community stronger and better.

African Culture

1. Africa not only fostered culture worthy of study, it produced cultures as glorious as those found in Europe.

2. In Brazil and the Caribbean Islands, which also had slavery, it is easier to recognize the continuity of African culture in the lives of Blacks today. The White South forced pressure on slaves to assimilate. Furthermore, a significantly higher proportion of slaves in the United States were born in America and not Africa. As a result, slaves in the United States were born American, not African culture.(Patterson,1977)

3. The survival of African culture among Black Americans can be most easily documented in folklore, religion, music and aspects of social organization. African culture, like any other culture, is not like clothing that can be taken off and thrown away. Many new cultures emerged as slaves drew upon the older culture of Africaand adapted it to their American situation. (Rawick, 1972)

4. Most of the distinctive aspects of Black life today originate in the poverty and segregation that could not destroy Africa's rich cultural traditions. (Schaefer)

Moreover, Dr. Karenga studied the culture of the Yourbas, the Ibos, the Ashantis, the Zulus, and other African tribes. Inspite of the diversity within each tribe's customs and traditions, each group celebrated the harvest festival. This festival consists of rewarding all tribal members for their teamwork during the year. Dr. Karenga incorporated many African customs, traditions, symbols and words from the Swahili language. He added an "a" to the Swahili word Kwanzaa, which means fruits of the harvest, to create the name for the holiday.

During different eras, William Edward Burghardt Dubois (1868-1963), Marcus Garvey (1887-1940) and Kwame Nkrumah (1909-1972), first prime minister of a newly-independent Ghana in 1957, were influential African Americans or African leaders advocating Pan-Africanism philosophy. Many scholars describe Pan-Africanism as an intellectual and cultural movement. It has two main goals: to foster unity among peoples of African descent across barriers of geography and language, and to celebrate the contributions of Africans to world history and civilization. According to the African American Desk Reference, during the 1960s, Pan-African ideas exerted a powerful influence on African Americans, prompting an upsurge in nationalism and Afrocentric ideas, a rejection of mainstream American culture, the adoption of African-related dress and hairstyles, and the demand for African and African American Studies programs. Kwanzaa represents the true spirit of Pan-Africanism. The model, values and practices are selected from all parts of African culture.

As with any group, connection to one's ancestral lineage is an important factor for preserving one's culture, or in this case, recapturing one's past. The demands for equality also heighten the need for self-identification particularly in naming. Some identify with African American because it recognizes the unique heritage of African Americans as products of both worlds. African American and Black are preferred labels for the majority of individuals of African descent residing in America. Therefore, African American and Black are used interchangeably.

During the '60s, the practice of claiming an African name began as an expression of Black pride. Another charismatic African American leader, Malcom X (1925-1962), formerly known as Malcolm Little, sought to create a new identity untainted by what he viewed as white racism, cultural genocide and control. In general, the Nation of Islam advocated replacing one's last name with an "X" to symbolize the renunciation of the "master's" name imposed on enslaved ancestors.

As Dr. Charles V. Hamilton (b. 1929), a professor of political science at Columbia University, said, "The whole business of names has been a constant troubling issue in the history of African Americans." Over the years, African Americans have been described in so many different ways– "Negroes," "New Negro," "colored people," "persons of color," "colored Americans," "Black Anglo-Saxons," "Afro-Americans"–that the sense of collective identity suffered in the process. While in search of self-identification, self-affirmation and self-determination, many former slaves became disenchanted with labels of "colored," "Negro" and "New Negro." W.E.B. DuBois addressed this issue in an article entitled, "The Name, 'Negro'" in The Crisis magazine. In 1928, a young man named Roland A. Barton, who took umbrage at the designation "Negro." Barton sent the following letter to the publisher explaining his perspective about name association with the identification of Americans of African heritage:

Dear Sir:

I am only a high school student in my Sophomore year, and have not the understanding of your college educated men. It seems to me that since The Crisis is the Official Organ of the National Association for the Advancement of Colored People, which stands for equality for all Americans, why would it designate and segregate us as "Negroes," and not as "Americans."

The most piercing thing that hurts me in this February Crisis, which forced me to write, was the notice that called the natives of Africa "Negroes," instead of calling them "Africans," or "natives."

The word "Negro," or "nigger," is a white man's word to make us feel inferior. I hope to be a worker for my race; that is why I wrote this letter. I hope that by the time I become a man that this word, "Negro," will be abolished.

W.E.B. DuBois responded:

Do not at the outset of your career make the all too common error of mistaking names for things. Names are only conventional signs for identifying things. Things are the reality that counts. If a thing is despised, either because of ignorance or because it is despicable, you will not alter matters by changing its name. If men despise Negroes, they will not despise them less if Negroes are called "colored" or "Afro-Americans."
W.E.B. DuBois: Basic Writings, "The 'Name'" in The Crisis, March 1928 (reprint edition, New York: Library of America, Literacy Classics of the United States 1986), pg. 1220.

The challenge of identifying and linking the African American heritage to its African underpinnings is an essential part of Black empowerment.

Unlike other groups, African Americans are the only group to experience an American phenomenon, the Enslavement.

As previously mentioned, today, many Americans of African descent refer to themselves as Black or African American. However, African American is becoming the preferred choice because for many people of African descent it represents the interconnectedness to the ancestral past and present Americanization. Those in favor of identifying as African American argue that "Black" has been declared too general a term of racial designation that lacks cultural, historical or political links to Africa. Others argue that to young children "Black" is foremost a color, not an abstract racial category. For children to be told that they are Black when they can see for themselves that they are not, can be quite puzzling.

Yet some Blacks particularly those who are products of families that were members of the Black Panther party or activists in the Black Power movement, prefer Black because of linguistic simplicity. Many of my students point out that African American lacks emotional impact. Besides, it places Africa before America, which is the most immediate homeland. Whereas, being Black provokes compassion, speaking directly to the heart.

In the media during the past decade, the use of African American has become more politically acceptable than Black. Also, this is evident in formal contexts such as books, articles, lectures, and news reports.

Dr. Maulana Dabezitha Karenga

Malcom X

Martin Luther King, Jr.

W.E.B. DuBois

INSTITUTIONALIZATION OF SOCIAL AND POLITICAL CONDITIONING

This section includes an introduction to the historic institutionalization of social conditioning and political sanctioning of second class citizenship. The following information exemplifies the socialization process and the impact a caste system disguised in the Slave Codes, Jim Crow policies, and legislation.

Robert T. Schaefer writes:

Slave Codes, also known as Black Codes, were enforced during the enslavement and later replaced by Jim Crow social policies that denied African Americans basic humanity. Although the rules varied from state to state and from time to time, and were not always enforced, the more common features show the complete subjugation of the African slaves.

1. A slave could not marry or even meet with a free Black.

2. Marriage between slaves was not legally recognized

3. A slave could not buy or sell anything unless by special arrangement.

4. A slave could not possess weapons or liquor.

5. A slave could not quarrel with or use abusive language with whites.

6. A slave could not possess property (including money), except as allowed by his or her master.

7. A slave could make no will, nor could he or she inherit anything.

8. A slave could not make a contract or hire himself or herself out.

9. Slaves could not leave the plantation without a pass noting their destination and time of return.

10. No one, including whites, were to teach slaves (and in some areas even free Blacks), to read or write, or to give them books, including the Bible.

11. Slaves could not gamble and had to obey established curfews.

12. A slave could not testify except against another slave.

(Elkins,Franklin,Stamp)

"One of the strangest things about the career of Jim Crow, was that the system was born in the North and reached an advanced age, before moving South in force."(Woodward, 1974, pp. 17-19.)

The following landmark cases show the interrelatedness of the legal system toward the socialization of its citizens. Our legal system can either negatively or positively influence attitudes and behaviors in the larger community.

Dred Scott vs. Sanford 1857 created the legal stage of second class citizenship for African Americans. This case concerned a slave who was taken by his master into territory were slavery was forbidden by the Missouri Compromise. Dred Scott argued that he was no longer a slave because of his new residency. U.S. Supreme Court Chief Justice B. Taney, however ruled that the Missouri Compromise was void and that Congress had no power over territories except to prepare for their admission to the Union. Taney further stated that slaves were private property and had no rights, and even questioned whether they were human. This ruling erased any ground that African Americans were making toward equal citizenship.

In 1896 in the case of Plessy vs. Ferguson, the U.S. Supreme Court upheld the constitutionality of "separate, but equal" accommodations for African Americans. Originally in reference to seating in a railroad car, the ruling was quickly extended to the schools. The practical significance of this ruling was to add federal sanction to the legal separation of African American school children from white children, most notably in the South, for nearly 60 years. The impact of this ruling served to encourage discrimination and racial bias toward African Americans and offered them less than equal education.

In the precedent-shattering case of Brown vs. Board of Education of Topeka 1954, the U.S. Supreme Court states that separate educational facilities are inherently unequal. This decision influenced African Americans in a way that changed their existence. They now could attend schools that previously only white children were allowed to attend.

From the Smithsonian Institution's National Museum of African American History and Culture: Enslaved Peoples Narratives and the Smithsonian (Julia Blakely, Feb. 28, 2019) https://youtu. be/F2oqbab4VzQ–age-restrictedvideo

THE ADOPTION OF THE SWAHILI LANGUAGE

Recapturing lost African cultures and traditions includes recapturing language. Swahili is believed to be derived from Kiswahili. Frequently, they are used interchangeably. Swahili language was chosen for Kwanzaa because it encompasses a large portion of the Africa continent. Swahili is spoken by an estimated 50 million people and, after Arabic, is the most widely understood language in Africa.

There is much disagreement over the interpretation of the historical evidence for Swahili. Some scholars suggest that Swahili is an old language. African scholar Abdurahman Juma, who revised an article, "A Brief History of the Swahili Language," written by Hassan O. Ali, suggests that:

"The earliest known document recounting the past situation on the East African coast was written in the 2nd Century AD (in Greek language by an anonymous author at Alexandria in Egypt). It is called the *Periplus of Erythraean Sea* and says that time from Southern Arabia, used to speak with the natives in their local language, and they intermarried with them. Those that suggest that Swahili is an old language, point to this early source for the possible antiquity of the Swahili language."

The Colonial Period in Africa promoted the need for a common language. After Independence during the 1960s, Swahili was poised to emerge as the most dynamic modern language of Africa. Swahili is credited as the language of choice for those who carried through the program of standardization in the 1930s and 1940s, to enable the politicians of the 1950s to use it as the language of national unity. Swahili is an expressive, musical language, and one of the most popular languages in Africa. Swahili is the official language of Tanzania and Kenya, and is used extensively in Uganda and the eastern provinces of Zaire. It is also used in most of the East and Central African countries of Uganda, Zaire, Malawi, Rwanda, and the Congo.

The language Swahili has become the most widely known, taught, discussed and spoken African language on the Continent and the national language of the United Republic of Tanzania. (Whiteley)

The expansion of Swahili in land from the coast falls in to two phases: in the first, from about 1800 to 1850, the country was gradually opened up by trading caravans, who took the language with them in the form of a Swahili- speaking 'managerial' core. During the second phase, from around 1850 until the advent of the Colonial Powers, the first systematic studies of the language were made and used as a basis for teaching others. (Whiteley) Kiswahili or Swahili is the fastest growing African language. Also, there are controversial theories of the origin and development of Kiswahili in trade, religion and politics in East and Central Africa. Its origin has been debated by historians and linguists, and remains highly disputable. According to African scholars, former Prime Minister of Tanganyika, Julius Nyerere, is credited with the adoption of Swahili as a national language. Domestically, in 1964 in Tanzania, he inaugurated three reforms: a political system based on the principle of the one-party state, an economic system based on an African approach to socialism (what is called ujamaa or familyhood), and a cultural system based on the Swahili language. (Worldview)

The cultural policy based on Kiswahili was the earliest and the most durable. Tanganyika (and later Tanzania) became one of the few African countries to use an indigenous language in Parliament and as the primary language of national business. Kiswahili was increasingly promoted in politics, administration, education and the media. It became a major instrument of nation-building–and nation-building became the most lasting of Nyerere's legacies. (Worldview)

African scholar Ali Mazuri further writes:

"Nyerere's policies of making Kiswahili the national language of Tanzania deepened the sense of Tanzania's national consciousness and cultural pride. Parliament in Dar es Salaam debated exclusively in Kiswahili. Government business was increasingly conducted in Kiswahili. The mass media turned away from English in favor of Kiswahili. Newspapers had not only letters to the editor, but also poems to the editor in Kiswahili. And the educational system was experiencing the stresses and strains of competing claims of English and Kiswahili. Nyerere's translation of two of Shakespeare's plays into Kiswahili was done not because he 'loved Shakespeare less, but because he loved Kiswahili more.' He translated Shakespeare into Kiswahili partly to demonstrate that the Swahili language was capable of carrying the complexities of a genius of another civilization."

The dialect of Swahili referred to as Standard Swahili was established in 1930 by the Inter Territorial Language Committee and was based on the coastal dialect of Zanzibar, Kunguja.

Swahili is taught in many parts of the world. Over 40 institutions in the USA offer courses in Swahili (Linguistic Society of America, 1992). Major research centers in East Africa include the Institute of Swahili Research at the University of Dar es Salaam, and a similar institute in Zanzibar. Other efforts are made throughout the world to include Swahili in education curriculum for higher institutions of learning.

Basically a Bantu language, its proper name is Kiswahili, meaning "the language of the Coast." The alphabet consists of 24 letters. There is no sound for Q or X in the language. Swahili vowels are pronounced as follows:

a is pronounced like the "a" in far or in father
e is pronounced like the "a" as in day or in pay
i is pronounced like the "ee" in see or in free
o is pronounced like toe or in go
u is pronounced like the "oo" in coo or in too

Vowels are pronounced similar to those of Spanish. Consonants with only a few exceptions are pronounced the same way they are in English. "G" has a hard sound as in give. "R" is like the Spanish "R," and is made by rolling the tongue. General practice suggests placing the accent on the next-to-last syllable in most words, unless otherwise indicated. (See Appendix for a glossary of Swahili terms.)

THE TRADITIONS OF KWANZAA

Kwanzaa is celebrated from Dec. 26 to Jan. 1. Kwanzaa, which means "first fruits of the harvest" in the African language Kiswahili, has gained tremendous acceptance. It has become an important holiday, first in America. Since its founding in 1966 by Dr. Maulana Karenga, it has come to be observed by more than 15 million people worldwide, as reported in The New York Times. It is now celebrated by millions of people the world over – in the United States, Europe, Canada, the Caribbean, and parts of Africa.

There are also seven symbols depicted on a mat on which the other symbolic items rest: fruit and vegetables representing the harvest; a unity cup,from which all drink; a candle holder with seven candles, one black, three red and three green. (Green candles symbolize hope and the green earth, thered candles symbolize the blood of the African diaspora, and the one black candle symbolizes solidarity among Black people. On the first night of Kwanzaa, the black candle is lit; the second, red; the third, green, alternating from left to right until all the candles are lit by Jan.1. The family talks about the seven principles that day. Each candle represents one of the seven principles of Kwanzaa. An ear of corn is given for each child in the home, along with other gifts from the parents to the child. Optional items include the African American flag and a map of the motherland.

THE LIBATION STATEMENT

Kwanzaa, celebrated for seven days from Dec. 26 through Jan. 1, is a unique African American celebration with the focus on the traditional African values of family, community responsibility, commerce, and self-improvement.

Kwanzaa is neither political nor religious and, despite some misconceptions, it is not a substitute for Christmas. It simply reaffirms African-American people, their ancestors and culture. Kwanzaa, which means "fruits of the harvest" in Kiswahili, should be celebrated as a holiday of shared harvest, shared memories and shared beliefs. Many African Americans are reminded that while they are Americans, their roots are in Africa, the motherland. It is based on Nguzo Saba or the seven guiding principles that teach values to be practiced every day, not just during the Kwanzaa season.

NGUZO SABA (Seven Principles)

December 26 – Umoja (OO-MO-JAH)
Unity stresses the importance of togetherness for the family and the community, which is reflected in the African saying, "I am We" or "I am because We are."

December 27 – Kujichagulia (KOO-GEE-CHA-GOO-LEE-YAH)
Self-determination requires that we define our common interests and make decisions that are in the best interest of our family and community.

December 28 – Ujima (OO-GEE-MAH)
Collective work and responsibility remind us of our obligation to the past, presentandfuture,andthatwehavearoletoplayinthecommunity, societyandworld.

December 29 – Ujamma (OO-JAH-MAH)
Cooperative economics emphasizes our collective economic strength and encourages us to meet common needs through mutual support.

December 30 – Nia (NEE-YAH)
Purpose encourages us to look within ourselves and to set personal goals that are beneficial to the community.

December 31 – Kuumba (KOO-OOM-BAH)
Creativity makes use of our creative energies to build and maintain a strong and vibrant community.

January1 – Imani (EE-MAH-NEE)
Faith focuses on honoring the best for our traditions, draws upon the best in ourselves, and helps us to strive for a higher level of life for humankind by affirming our self-worth and confidence in our ability to succeed and triumph in a righteous struggle.

Traditionally, many groups pour the libation in remembrance of their ancestors on special occasions. The Kwanzaa libation statement provides an opportunity to reflect upon the African past and American present. The symbol of water is used because it represents the essence of life. The libation should be placed in a communal cup and poured in the direction of the four winds: north, south, east and west. Then it should be passed among family members and guests who may either sip from the cup or make a sipping gesture.

> *For the Motherland cradle of civilization.*
> *For the ancestors and their indomitable spirit.*
> *For the elders from whom we can learn so much.*
> *For our youth who represent the promise for tomorrow.*
> *For our struggle and in remembrance of those who have struggled on our behalf.*
> *For Umoja, the principle of unity which should guide us in all that we do.*
> *For the creator who provides all things great and small.*

Gifts (Zawadi)

During Kwanzaa, gifts may be exchanged. It is suggested that gifts are handmade or functional, such as a book. However, it is suggested that they not be given if they create undue hardship or expense.

Karamu (Community Festival)

Kwanzaa closes with a community festival – Karamu. During the festival, family and friends welcome the new year with music, dancing and traditional dishes derived from African cuisine.

APPENDIX

A. Swahili Glossary of Kwanzaa Terms

Bendera (*ben-der-ra*)–National Black Liberation Flag
The bendera is black, red and green, and is similar to one that was first made popular by Marcus Garvey. Black is for the color of the people, red is for the struggle that is carried on by Africans and African-Americans for a better life, and green is for the future that will result from the struggle.

Habarigani (*ha-ba-rigani*)
A Swahili terms that means "What's the news?"

Harambee (*har-ram-be*)
A Swahili word that means "Let's all pull together."

Karamu (*kar-ra-mu*)
This is the feast that is held on the evening of Dec. 31.

Kikombe cha umoja (*ke-kom-bechau-mo-ja*)
The unity cup. This cup is passed in honor of the family ancestors, and as a sign of unity.

Kinara (*kin-na-ra*)
A candle holder. A symbol of our African ancestors, the root from which the family evolved.

Kuchunguza tenana kutoa ahadi tena (*ku-chu-ngu-zaten-nanaku-toa-haditen-na*)
The speech that helps the audience to remember the things Kwanzaa teaches.

Kukumbuka (*ku-kum-bu-ka*)
Short speech by a member of the audience on the meaning of Kwanzaa.

Kukaribishna (*ku-kar-i-bi-sha*)
The welcoming ceremony that is held at the beginning of the Karamu feast.

Kushangilia (*ku-shan-gi-lia*)
To rejoice.

Kutoamjina (*ku-toama-ji-na*)
The calling of the names of the family ancestors, as well as African-American heroes and heroines.

Kuumba (*ku-um-ba*)
One of the seven principles of Kwanzaa. It means "creativity" in Swahili.

Kwanzaa (*kwan-za*)
The term means "first" in Swahili.

Kwanzaa(*kwan-za)*
A cultural holiday created in 1966 by Dr. Maulana Karenga.

Libation statement – The speech that is made before passing the communal unity cup (kikombechaumoja).

Mazao (*ma-za-o*) – The word means crops. A bowl of fruit and vegetables is placed on a mat, the mkeka, to represent the rewards of working together.

Mishumaasaba (*mi-shu-ma-asa-ba*)

The term refers to the seven candles of Kwanzaa.Three red candles, one black candle (in the center), then three green candles are placed in the kinara. Each candle represents one of the Nguzo Saba (seven principles) of Kwanzaa.

Mkeka mat (*m-ke-ka*)
The mkeka is a symbol for unity and represents a firm foundation to build on. All the symbols of Kwanzaa are placed on the mkeka.

Muhindi (*mu-hin-di*)
The ears of corn that are used to represent children during Kwanzaa.

Nguzo Saba (*n-gu-zo sa-ba*)

A term that means "seven principles" in Swahili. The Nguzo Saba is the guide for daily living. This guide is studied during Kwanzaa to be practiced throughout the year.

Ngoma (*n-go-ma*)
The drum performance given during the karamu feast.

Swahili (*swa-hi-li*)
A nontribal African language used in many parts of Africa.

Tamshi la tambiko (*tam-shilatam-bi-ko*)
The libation speech that is read before passing the unity cup.

Tamshilatutaonana (*tam-shilatu-ta-o-na-na*)
The farewell speech that is given at the end of the karamu feast.

Zawadi (*za-wa-di*)
The gifts given during Kwanzaa as a reward for the commitment made and kept during the holiday.

B.

Yo! What's Kwanzaa
–Abiodun Oyewole, Dec. 23, 1987

Kwanzaa is a holiday for seven days

With seven laws to learn

In seven different ways

Now the language is Swahili

And it's plan to see

This is an African connection

To Bring Unity

Kwanzaa means first fruits

Of the harvest time

Now we may not own a garden

But we've got our minds

Plant the seeds in our head

That we can grow at will

Cultivate and educate

Until it's time to chill

Nguzo Saba means the seven laws

And each one is on a mission

For a righteous cause

C.

Seven Principles

– Bernice Johnson Reagon

Umoja – Unity That Brings Us Together

Umoja – Unity That Brings Us Together

Umoja – Unity That Brings Us Together

Kuujichagalia – Kuujichagalia – Kuujichagalia

Kuujichagalia – We Will Determine Who We Are

Kuujichagalia – We Will Determine Who We Are

Kuujichagalia – We Will Determine Who We Are

Ujima – Working And Building Our Union

Ujima – Working And Building Our Union

Ujima – Working And Building Our Union

Ujamaa – We'll Spend Our Money Wisely

Ujamaa – We'll Spend Our Money Wisely

Ujamaa – We'll Spend Our Money Wisely

Nia – We Know The Purpose Of Our Lives

Nia – We Know The Purpose Of Our Lives

Nia – We Know The Purpose Of Our Lives

Kuumba – All That We Touch Is More Beautiful

Kuumba – All That We Touch Is More Beautiful

Kuumba – All That We Touch Is More Beautiful

Imani – We Believe That We Can

        We Know That We Can

          We Will Any Way

            That We Can

BIBLIOGRAPHY

Asante, Molefi. *The Afro-Centric Idea*. Philadelphia: Temple University Press, 1987.

Ashton, E.P. 1944 *Swahili Grammar* (Including Intonation). London: Longman.

Awolalu, Omosade J. *Yoruba Beliefs and Sacrificial Rites*. London: Longman, 1879, p. 143ff.

Coursey, D.G. *The New Yam Festival Among the Ewe*, Ghana Notes and Queries. 10 (December) 1968.

Cooper, Anna Julia, *A Voice From the South*. New York: Oxford University Press, 1988, p. 60.

Dewart, Janet. *The State of Black America 1991*. The National Urban League, Inc. January, 1991.

Fanon, Frantz. *The Wretched of the Earth*. New York: Grove Press, 1968, p. 167.

Hassan-El, Kashif Malik. *The Willie Lynch Letter and The Making of a Slave*. Chicago: Lushena Books, 1999.

Harrison, Maureen & Gilbert, Steve Ed. *Civil Rights Decisions of the United State Supreme Court: The 19th Century*. San Diego: Excellent Books, USA, 1994.

> *Civil Rights Decisions of the United States Supreme Court: The Twentieth Century.*

Frankfort, Henri. *Kingship and the Gods*. Chicago: University of Chicago Press, 1948, p.18 ff.

Hinnebusch, T.J. 1979, *Swahili*. In T. Shopen, ed. Languages and Their Status. Cambridge, MA: Winthrop, pp. 209-293.

Junrod, Henri. *The Life of a South African Tribe*. New York: University Books, 1966, vol. 1, p. 401.

Karenga, Maulana, *Black Studies and the Problematic of Paradigm*. Journal of Black Studies, 18, 4 (June) 1988, p. 404.

> *Kawaida Theory: An Introductory Outline*. Los Angeles: University of Sankore Press.

> *Kwanzaa: Origin, Concept, Practice*. Los Angeles: Kawaida Publications, 1977, 1984, pp. 18 62ff.

Linguistic Society of America. 1992. *Directory of Programs in Linguistics in the United States and Canada*: 1993. Washington, D.C.

Mends, E.H., *Ritual in the Social Life of Ghanaian Society in J.M. Assimeng* (ed.), *Traditional Life, Culture and Literature in Ghana*. New York: Cinch Magazine Limited, 1976, p. 8.

The National Peace Corps Association. Worldview Fall 1999 vol. 12 no.4

Nurse, D. and Hinnebusch, T.J. *Swahili and Sabaki: A Linguistic History*. Berkeley and Los Angeles: University of California Press, 1993.

Nyerere, Julius. *Freedom and Socialism/Uhuruna Sujamaa*. New York: Oxford University Press,1969, p.316.

Sarpong, Peter. *The Sacred Stools of the Akan*. Accra-Tema: Ghana Publishing Company,1971, pp. 66ff.

Schaefer, Robert T. *Racial and Ethnic Groups. 4th ed.* New York: Scott, Foresman. 1990.

Schomburg Center. *African-American Desk Reference*. Toronto: John Wiley, 1999.

Steer, Edward, Revised and partly rewritten by A.B. Hellier. *Swahili Exercises*. Oxford University Press in association with Sheldon Press, 1976.

Wald, B. *Swahili and Bantu Languages*. In B. Comrie, ed. The World's Major Language. pp. 1991-1014. New York: Oxford University Press, 1987.

Whiteley, Wilfred. *Swahili: The Rise of a National Language*. London: Methuen & Co. Ltd., 1969.

Zawawi, S. *Kishwalli Kwa Kitendo: An Introductory Course.*New York: Harper & Row, 1971.

SPECIAL THANKS

Roger A. Ramsammy, Ph.D.
President

Hudson Valley Community College Board of Trustees
Neil J. Kelleher, '91
Chairman

I also wish to thank the original reviewer, Susan McDermott, emeritus associate professor of English, who provided many helpful comments and suggestions for the first Kwanzaa Fact Book in 2000. I also acknowledge Sue Grayson, retired faculty librarian, for her research assistance, and the late Anthony Walsh,a retired professor who provided research on the Swahili language. Lastly, thanks to Deborah Gardner in the communications office for help with the second edition of the Kwanzaa Fact Book and promoting Sisters In Cynch Club Edu-Dramas.

To my students at Hudson Valley Community College, thanks for caring and allowing me to share a celebration of the African American culture.

As part of the faculty and staff, we recognize that all people from various racial and ethnic backgrounds are part of the human family sharing a variety of expressions of an indefinite number of dimensions of human qualities and characteristics in constant dynamic interaction.

www.ingramcontent.com/pod-product-compliance
Lightning Source LLC
Chambersburg PA
CBHW032104020426
42335CB00011B/487